Mother Goose Phonics

BY DEBORAH SCHECTER

SCHOLASTIC
PROFESSIONAL BOOKS

NEW YORK • TORONTO • LONDON • AUCKLAND • SYDNEY
MEXICO CITY • NEW DELHI • HONG KONG

For my sisters,
Gail and Diane,
in memory of our mother,
Charlotte

Front cover and interior design by Kathy Massaro
Cover photos by Donnelly Marks
Cover and interior illustrations by Maxie Chambliss

ISBN # 0-439-12927-3
Copyright © 1999 by Deborah Schecter
All rights reserved.
Printed in the U.S.A.

Contents

About This Book

Teaching Phonics With Mother Goose

"Hickory, Dickory, Dock"..."Little Bo-Peep"..."Twinkle, Twinkle, Little Star"... these and other beloved nursery rhymes have delighted children for generations. Rhythmic and playful, nursery rhymes are a natural motivator for teaching phonics to young children and helping them gain confidence as readers. Each of the nursery rhymes included in this book forms the basis for a lesson on a key phonics skill. The fun-filled activities, games, and manipulatives are inviting ways to help children recognize the sound-letter relationships and spelling patterns in words, setting them on the path to becoming fluent readers. So get ready to see rhyme-rich phonics in action as children stock Mother Hubbard's cupboard with rhyming words, climb the Hickory Dickory Consonant Clock, plant a short- and long-vowel garden for Mistress Mary, and practice *l*-blends as they help Mary's little lamb find its way to school.

Whether the children in your class are familiar with these timeless verses or are experiencing them for the first time, the nursery rhymes and activities in *Mother Goose Phonics* are sure to spark smiles and laughter and foster a love of reading.

What's Inside

Here's an overview of the features you'll find in the lessons in this book.

Nursery Rhyme Each ready-to-reproduce rhyme has large, easy-to-read print and delightful illustrations.

Skill See at a glance the phonics focus in a particular lesson.

Materials Use this handy, complete list to gather the materials needed for each lesson.

Getting Ready Setup instructions, easy how-to's, and helpful tips are provided to ensure that activities go smoothly.

Reading the Rhyme These ideas, strategies, and mini-lessons help you use the nursery rhyme to teach a key phonics skill.

Activity Give children practice in a specific phonics skill with these fun, interactive games, activities, and manipulatives. Many include easy patterns and game boards that are ready to be reproduced.

Extending Learning These engaging pocket chart activities, interactive bulletin boards, games, and other activities provide additional opportunities to reinforce the lesson.

Mother Goose Learning Center Inviting, independent and small-group activities encourage children to continue working with the sound-letter relationships in words.

More Phonics Fun This section highlights other phonics skills to teach with a particular rhyme and other nursery rhymes that can be used to teach the same phonics skill.

Mother Goose Book Nook Here you'll find suggestions for classic renditions of particular nursery rhymes as well as new versions to enhance your lessons.

Helpful Hints

Reading the Rhymes

To enrich children's reading experience, use the following suggestions and strategies with any of the nursery rhymes in this book.

⭐ Write the rhymes in large print on chart paper, then laminate so that they can be reused. Use different colored wipe-off markers to highlight, for example, rhyming words, words with long vowels, or words that begin with a particular consonant blend.

⭐ Give each child a copy of the nursery rhyme to follow as you read aloud. Later, children will enjoy reading the rhyme independently or taking it home to share with family members.

Mary Had a Little Lamb

Mary had a little lamb,
Its fleece was white as snow.
And everywhere that Mary went,
The lamb was sure to go.

It followed her to school one day,
Which was against the rules.
It made the children laugh and play
To see a lamb at school.

Mother Goose Book Nook

The following collections include familiar versions and new twists on favorite nursery rhymes to enjoy with your class.

Animal Nursery Rhymes selected by Angela Wilkes (Dorling Kindersley, 1992). Fascinating, close-up photos of different animals enhance the rhymes in this handsome collection.

- - - - - - - -

Each Peach Pear Plum by Janet and Allan Ahlberg (Viking, 1979). In this delightful book, young readers will have fun playing "I Spy" as they look for Mother Goose characters hidden within the playful and detailed illustrations.

- - - - - - - -

Finger Rhymes edited and illustrated by Marc Tolon Brown (Dutton, 1980). Clear, easy-to-follow illustrations make it easy to learn the fingerplay movements to 14 favorite nursery rhymes.

continued on next page

Mother Goose Book Nook

continued from previous page

Mother Goose illustrated by Scott Cook (Knopf, 1994). Colorful oil paintings illustrate 60 nursery rhymes with exuberance, whimsy, and lavish detail.

Mother Goose by Wendy Watson (Lothrop, Lee & Shepard, 1989). Handy indexes by first line and subject are a helpful addition to this appealing and extensive collection.

My Very First Mother Goose by Iona Opie (Candlewick, 1996). Winsome and appealing watercolors by Rosemary Wells illustrate this charming collection of nearly 70 nursery rhymes.

The New Adventures of Mother Goose: Gentle Rhymes for Happy Times created by Bruce Lansky (Meadowbrook Press, 1993). These silly and delightful updates of classic nursery rhymes are sure to tickle children's funny bones.

continued on next page

★ When reading a rhyme for the first time, ask children if they are familiar with it. Then read it aloud several times. Invite children to respond to the rhyme and discuss unfamiliar vocabulary. Then ask them to join in with you for a rereading. Volunteers or pairs of children might then want to take turns reading different lines aloud.

★ Challenge children to listen for rhyming words. (For example, *clock* and *dock* in "Hickory, Dickory, Dock," and *shoe* and *do* in "The Old Woman Who Lived in a Shoe.") Guide children to notice that rhyming words can have similar and different spelling patterns.

★ Once children are familiar with a particular nursery rhyme, invite them to anticipate the rhymes in upcoming lines. Also encourage them to substitute real or nonsense rhyming words to create their own personalized versions.

★ Photocopy additional copies of the rhymes, masking out key words. For example, for "Humpty Dumpty," you might omit the word *wall* from the line "Humpty Dumpty sat on a wall" and ask children to fill in the blank with other words that rhyme with *wall*. You can also use self-sticking notes to cover key words on the poems written on chart paper.

★ Use the rhymes to help children focus on different phonics skills. For example, as you read aloud a poem, you might ask children to listen for all the words that begin or end with a specific letter or sound.

★ Invite children to learn the traditional melodies to different nursery rhymes (or make up their own) to help them recognize rhyming patterns and build phonemic awareness and word recognition. Introduce children to some of these traditional melodies with the following songbooks and audiotapes:

● *Jane Yolen's Mother Goose Songbook* (Boyds Mill Press, 1992).

● *Mother Goose* audiotape; Celeste Holm, Boris Karloff, and Cyril Ritchard lend their singing talents to more than 70 nursery rhymes set to music (Caedmon/Harper Audio, 1992; 800-331-3761).

● *Mother Goose & Nursery Rhyme* audiotape and book (Production Associates; 800-535-8368).

● *Mother Goose Songbook* by Tom Glazer (Doubleday, 1990).

● *Wee Sing Nursery Rhymes and Lullabies* by Pamela Conn Beall and Susan Hagen Nipp (Putnam, 1986; 800-847-5515).

Wonderful Reading Wands

It's helpful to use a pointer to call attention to specific words and to track the print as you read the rhymes with children. Why not make fanciful reading wands to enhance the reading experience! All you need are 12-inch dowels, a hot glue gun, and some simple supplies. With "Twinkle, Twinkle, Little Star," for example, you might hot-glue a glittery or glow-in-the-dark star to the end of a dowel. For "The Itsy Bitsy Spider," a wiggly plastic spider would be just the thing! Color the dowel with a broad-tip marker or wrap it with ribbon, gluing the end in place.

Pocket Chart Rhymes

Copy each line of a rhyme onto a sentence strip. Once children are familiar with the rhyme, mix up the strips and place them in the pocket chart so the rhyme is out of order. Invite volunteers to unscramble the rhyme and put the lines in correct sequence.

Encourage children to use sequencing vocabulary, such as *first, second, third,* and *last,* as they reorder the strips. Then put the sets of strips in a learning center for independent practice, numbering them on the back to make them self-checking.

As an added challenge, cut a sentence strip into individual words, and invite children to reorder the phrase or sentence or slot in new words.

On small index cards, draw pictures or use stickers or pictures from old workbooks to illustrate words in a rhyme. As children read the poem aloud with you, invite volunteers to come up to the pocket chart and place each picture beside the word it illustrates.

My Mother Goose Books

Let children create a collection of the reproducible nursery rhymes in this book. Give each child an 11- by 17-inch piece of construction paper or tagboard, folded in half. Invite children to decorate the cover of their book and title it "My Mother Goose Book." Children can then insert the poems and bind their book with staples, brass fasteners, ribbon, or yarn.

Mother Goose Book Nook

continued from previous page

The Real Mother Goose illustrated by Blanche Fisher Wright (Scholastic, 1993). Colorful illustrations with an old-fashioned flavor accompany more than 160 classic nursery rhymes.

Rhymes & Reasons: An Annotated Collection of Mother Goose Rhymes by James C. Christensen (Greenwich Workshop Press, 1997). Intricate paintings depict 72 nursery rhymes accompanied by notes about their origins. Includes a colorful wall poster.

Visit the Web site of the Mother Goose Society (www.gbalc.org/ MotherGooseSociety/ index.html) for information about the origin of different nursery rhymes as well as recipes, games, and activities.

Pat-a-Cake

Pat-a-cake, pat-a-cake,
Baker's man,
Bake me a cake as fast as you can.
Pat it and prick it
And mark it with a T.
Put it in the oven
For Tommy and me.

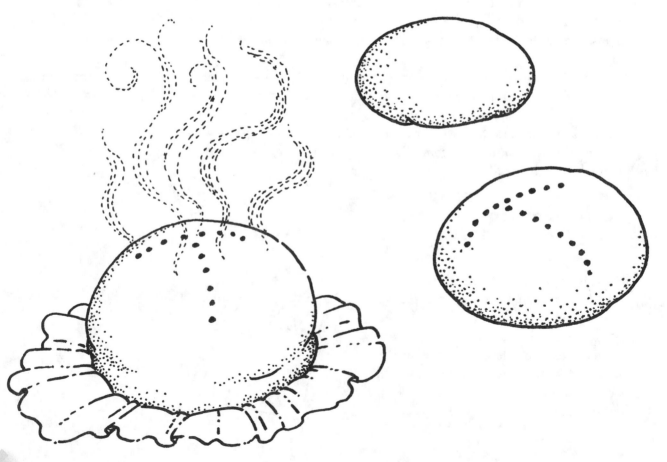

Pat-a-Cake

Getting Ready

1 Photocopy the poem on page 8 for each child, and write the poem on chart paper. Highlight the letter *T* and the name *Tommy* by printing them in a different color or by underlining them.

2 List children's names in alphabetical order on chart paper, underlining the first letter in each name. (If several children have names beginning with the same letter, simply list these one after the other.) Supply examples for any missing letters. See the suggestions on page 10.

Reading the Rhyme

1 Read aloud the rhyme, tracking the print as you read. Then reread it, inviting children to pantomine the action. Model how to trace the letter *T* on your hand when you read the phrase "and mark it with a T."

2 Ask children to identify the name mentioned in the rhyme (Tommy) and the sound and letter it begins with /t/*t*. Ask: "Do you know other names or words that begin with this sound?" (Tamika, Tina, Todd, Tony) Write these names and words on the list and underline the letter *T*.

3 Reread the rhyme and use self-sticking notes to substitute the *T* and *Tommy* with children's first initials and names. Fill in any missing letters. As you read the rhyme again, invite children to trace the substitute letter on their hand when you say it.

Alphabet Cakes

1 Hand out a copy of the pattern page to each child. Have children cut out the cake patterns, line them up (with the outside on top), and punch holes as indicated. Provide yarn to tie the books together.

2 Tell children to mark the outside of their cake with their first initial and write their name. Inside, have them write other names and words (or draw pictures of things) that begin with the same letter. Then invite children to color their cakes and decorate with glitter and other art supplies.

SKILLS

alphabet recognition, sound-letter correspondence, alphabetical order

MATERIALS

★ chart paper
★ markers
★ self-sticking notes
★ hole punch

For each child:

★ Alphabet Cake patterns, page 11
★ scissors
★ crayons, markers, glitter, and other art supplies
★ 6-inch piece of yarn or ribbon

Names From A to Z

A	Ann
B	Billy
C	Carlos
D	Dylan
E	Ed
F	Fran
G	Gwen
H	Harriet
I	Inez
J	Jackie
K	Kathy
L	Larry
M	Moesha
N	Nadia
O	Oliver
P	Peter
Q	Quentin
R	Raj
S	Seth
T	Tamika
U	Ulysses
V	Vincent
W	Wiley
X	Xanthe (ZAN-thee)
Y	Yolanda
Z	Zachary

3 Let children take turns sharing their cakes with classmates. Then create an ABC Word Wall for each letter of the alphabet, adding the words in children's books.

4 As a variation, instead of making name cakes, invite children to name and decorate the kind of cake they would bake, such as vanilla, chocolate, strawberry, and so on. On the outside of their cakes, have children write the first letter of the word, and on the inside, words that begin with the same letter.

Extending Learning

ABC Cake Line-Up Give children practice alphabetizing words. Review the alphabetical list of names on the chart paper. Then, using a tube of cake-decorating icing, label 26 round cookies with uppercase letters from *A* to *Z*. Prepare another set of cookies with lowercase letters from *a* to *z*. Cover a table with a paper tablecloth, then randomly set out the cookies labeled with the uppercase letters. Have children wash their hands and then take turns placing the "cakes" in a row, in alphabetical order. Repeat the activity using the lowercase labeled cookies. Then it's time for a tasty ABC snack!

ABC Read! Stock a bookshelf with alphabet books on different topics. Invite children to take turns choosing a book for you to read aloud. Let children choose words from the books to add to your ABC Word Wall.

Mother Goose Learning Center

Bake a Cake! Store children's alphabet cake books in a toy oven or cardboard box. Seal the box closed, then cut a flap in the side of the box to make a door. Use a marker to draw oven features such as knobs and door handles. When children come to the center, they can read and share classmates' cake books.

More Phonics Fun

Use the Pat-a-Cake rhyme to help children practice long- and short-vowel *a*. (Long- and short-*a* words in this rhyme include *cake, baker's, bake, pat, man, fast, can, and.*)

My

Cake

Name _____

Outside

Alphabet Cake

Inside

Cackle, Cackle, Mother Goose

Cackle, cackle, Mother Goose,
Have you any feathers loose?
Truly have I, pretty fellow,
Half enough to fill a pillow.
Here are quills, take one or two,
And down to make a bed for you.

Cackle, Cackle,
Mother Goose

Getting Ready

1 Photocopy the poem on page 12 for each child, and write the poem on chart paper.

2 Make two "pillowcases" that children will fill with feathers. For each one, fold the construction paper or fabric in half the short way. Staple the bottom and one side closed as shown. Leave the top open. (See the picture on page 14.)

3 For each playing group, make 26 copies of the feather pattern on page 14 and cut them out. Make a set of alphabet cards by writing one uppercase and one lowercase letter on each feather. If you like, glue a craft feather to the other side of each feather pattern.

Reading the Rhyme

1 Read aloud the nursery rhyme. Discuss words that might be unfamiliar to children, such as *quills* and *down*. (If possible, have on hand a sample of a real feather and down, or a feather pillow for children to see and touch.)

2 Display the alphabet feather card for the letter *f* and ask children to name the letter on the feather or the sound the letter stands for. Then challenge children to find a word in the nursery rhyme that begins with *f*. (*feather, fellow, fill*)

3 Repeat this process with other alphabet feather cards, including examples of vowels and consonants.

Fill the Feather Pillow!

1 Divide the class into two groups, or play with two smaller groups of 4–5 children. Give each team a "pillowcase."

2 Display an alphabet feather card to the first player on Team 1. Ask the child to name the letter or the sound the letter sounds for. Team players can help one another, but the first player must say the letter or sound.

SKILLS

alphabet recognition, sound-letter correspondence

MATERIALS

★ marker
★ chart paper

For each playing group:

★ two 8 1/2- by 11-inch sheets of white construction paper or pieces of fabric (a torn-up old sheet works well)
★ stapler
★ scissors
★ feather pattern, page 14
★ craft feathers and glue (optional)

3 If the player answers correctly, he or she keeps the feather and puts it in the team's pillow. If the answer is incorrect, the first player on Team 2 gets a turn.

4 The team that has the most feathers in their pillow after all the alphabet cards have been named is the winner.

Extending Learning

Fill the Pillow Another Way Scramble the cards and give each team half. Then say aloud words that begin with different letters. For example, /b/—*boy*. The first player must hold up the correct alphabet feather card. Again, team players can help one another, but the first player must hold up the card. If the answer is correct, the player puts the card in the pillow. Play continues until one team has placed all of its cards in the pillow.

Instead of using all 26 letters of the alphabet, make a set of consonant feather cards, making extra cards for the consonants most frequently found in words—*b, f, l, m, r, s, t.*

Mother Goose Learning Center

Sweet Dream Words Help children set up a cozy doll-size bedroom in a corner of your room, complete with a doll bed, pillow, sheets, quilt or blanket, rug, doll (with nightgown or pajamas), a soft night-light, and so on. Place a small piece of adhesive-backed Velcro on each object. Then write the names of each item on a small card, attach a piece of Velcro to the back, and place in a basket. Have children visit the center and match the word labels to the items in the mini-bedroom. Extend the experience by making a Bedtime Word Wall on a piece of chart paper. Invite children to add bedtime-related words, such as *dream, sleep, moon,* and so on.

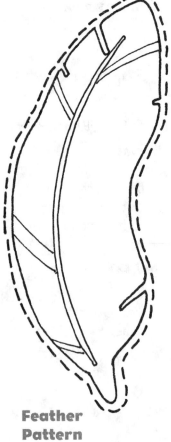

Feather Pattern

Old Mother Hubbard

Old Mother Hubbard went to the cupboard,
To give her poor dog a bone.

But when she got there, the cupboard was bare,
And so the poor dog had none.

She went to the baker's to buy him some bread,
And when she came back, the poor dog was fed.

She went to the hatter's to buy him a hat,
And when she came back, he was feeding the cat.

She went to the barber's to buy him a wig,
And when she came back, he was dancing a jig.

She went to the tailor's to buy him a coat,
And when she came back, he was riding a goat.

The dame made a curtsey,
The dog made a bow.
The dame said, "Your servant,"
The dog said, "Bow-wow!"

Old Mother Hubbard

MATERIALS

★ chart paper
★ marker

For each child:

★ cupboard pattern and word cards, pages 18–19
★ scissors
★ glue stick or tape
★ crayons or markers

Getting Ready

1 Photocopy the poem on page 15 for each child, and write the poem on chart paper.

2 Make a copy of both pattern pages for each child.

Reading the Rhyme

1 Read aloud the rhyme, verse by verse, stopping to discuss terms such as *hatter*, *dame*, and so on.

2 Reread the rhyme and ask children to listen for rhyming words. Help them by circling the words *hat* and *cat*. Ask: "How are these words alike?" (They both end in /at/; they both sound the same at the end.) Ask children if they can name other words that rhyme with *hat* and *cat*. (*sat, mat, fat*)

3 Circle another rhyming word pair, *bread/fed*. These words rhyme but have different spelling patterns. Invite children to find other rhyming word pairs, noting spelling similarities and differences.

4 "Old Mother Hubbard" is a fun rhyme for children to act out. Read the rhyme again, then invite pairs of children to take turns acting out each verse. Children may also enjoy having Old Mother Hubbard visit other places and inserting different rhyming word pairs. For example:

She went to the butcher's
To buy him a bone,
And when she came back,
He was on the phone.

She went to the candy store
To buy him some candy,
And when she came back,
He was doing just dandy.

Mother Hubbard's Rhyming Cupboard

1 Give children each the cupboard pattern and word card pages to cut out. Invite them to color the patterns, if they like. Then have children cut off the word-card strip and cut out the individual word cards. Blank word cards are provided for you to add additional rhyming words.

2 Show children how to cut open the doors to the cupboard along the dotted lines and fold them back. (An easy way to cut the doors is to fold the paper at a right angle to the dotted lines. Then snip along the lines from the crease of the fold inward.) Next, have children place the front of the cupboard on top of the inside and tape together.

3 Tell children that their job is to fill Mother Hubbard's cupboard with rhyming word "bones." Ask them to identify each of the pictures on the shelves. Then tell them to glue words that rhyme with each picture on the appropriate shelf.

Mother Goose Book Nook

Old Mother Hubbard and Her Wonderful Dog by James Marshall (Farrar, Straus & Giroux, 1991). Children will love the whimsical illustrations in this imaginative retelling.

....

Mother Hubbard's Christmas by John O'Brien (Boyds Mill Press, 1996). In this hilarious twist on the familiar rhyme, Old Mother Hubbard's dog is up to new tricks as Mother Hubbard tries to get ready for the holidays.

❖ Mother Goose Learning Center ❖

Mother Hubbard's Rhyming Word Wall On large sheets of construction paper, draw simple storefronts with the following labels: <u>Hat</u> Store, <u>Bread</u> Store, <u>Wig</u> Store, and <u>Coat</u> Store, underlining the first word on each. Tack these signs in a row on a bulletin board. Then, on small, unlined index cards, write rhyming words for *hat*, *bread*, *wig*, and so on. Place these in a basket beneath the board. Invite children to stock each store with rhyming words. Have them choose word cards from the basket and use pushpins to tack them to the store with the corresponding rhyme. Let children add other rhyming word cards to the center.

More Phonics Fun

"Old Mother Hubbard" offers lots of opportunities for children to learn words with long and short vowels; for example, *old, bone, coat, goat, dame, bread, fed,* and *hat.*

Mother Hubbard's Rhyming Cupboard

(Outside)

Mother Goose Phonics Scholastic Professional Books

mat float head dig cat boat

Mother Hubbard's Rhyming Cupboard

(Inside)

goat sat twig bed big red

Humpty Dumpty

Humpty Dumpty sat on a wall.
Humpty Dumpty had a great fall.
All the king's horses
And all the king's men
Couldn't put Humpty together again.

Humpty Dumpty

Getting Ready

1 Photocopy the poem on page 20 for each child, and write the poem on chart paper.

2 Make multiple copies of the game board and the puzzle pattern. Color if desired. Cut out the puzzle pieces and place each set in a plastic sandwich bag.

3 Fill in the game boards by selecting different words from each of the lists below. See example, bottom right. (You may wish to laminate the game boards and spinner first so they can be reused.)

den, pen, ten, then, when, hen, Ben, wren, Glen, Ken, yen

fall, all, call, hall, tall, ball, small, stall, Paul, haul, shawl

bring, cling, ring, sing, sling, spring, sting, string, swing, thing, wing

4 Copy and enlarge the spinner and assemble it with a brass fastener and paper clip as shown. In each section of the spinner, write one of the following words: *king, men, wall.*

Reading the Rhyme

1 Read aloud the rhyme, then invite children to join in as you reread it. Invite children to make up simple hand motions to act it out. (For example, they might make a fist to show Humpty when he is whole, then show him falling and spread out their fingers to show him breaking into pieces.)

2 Invite children to point out the rhyming words. Discuss the rhyming word pairs. Guide children to notice that *wall* and *fall* have the same spelling pattern, while *again* and *men* do not.

Humpty Dumpty Puzzle Game

1 Divide the class into playing groups of three. Give each player one game board and one set of puzzle pieces.

SKILL

rhyme

MATERIALS

★ chart paper
★ marker

For each playing group:

★ Humpty Dumpty game board and puzzle patterns, pages 23–24
★ scissors
★ 3 plastic sandwich bags
★ crayons or water-based markers
★ spinner pattern, page 22
★ brass fastener
★ small paper clip

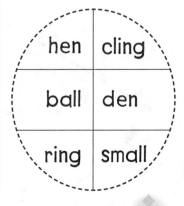

hen	cling
ball	den
ring	small

Humpty Dumpty: A Pop-Up Book illustrated by Moira Kemp and Steve Augarde (Lodestar, 1996). In this fanciful pop-up book, the king's horses and men fail Humpty Dumpty, but the king, queen, and a doctor come to the rescue with bandages and glue.

2 In turn, each player spins the spinner and states aloud a word, such as *wall*. The player then checks his or her game board to see if there is a word that rhymes with *wall*. If the player has a word that rhymes, he or she may place a puzzle piece over that word. If not, the next player takes a turn.

3 Play continues until all players have put Humpty together. Afterward, place the game in a learning center for independent practice. Use other words from "Humpty Dumpty" to make additional games. Suggestions follow:

sat: *mat, cat, fat, rat, hat, bat, chat, flat, pat, splat, that*

great: *ate, date, eight, gate, hate, late, plate, skate, wait, Kate, rate*

had: *add, bad, Chad, dad, fad, lad, mad, pad, sad, glad, plaid*

Mother Goose Learning Center

Rhyming Word Eggs Use plastic Easter eggs to create another Humpty Dumpty rhyming game. Write one word from a set of rhyming words on a self-adhesive label and affix to the outside of a plastic egg. Write rhyming words on slips of paper and place in a small basket. Repeat this process with two more eggs, using two other sets of rhyming words. Then set the eggs on a "wall." (Cut the bottom of an egg carton in half, the long way. Turn one half upside down and place the other half on top of it. Set an egg in every other cup.) Have children match the rhyming words with the correct egg. When they find a match, children put the slips of paper into that egg. To make the activity more challenging, use six eggs instead of three.

Game Board Spinner

More Phonics Fun

Use "Humpty Dumpty" to explore words with short vowels. Examples in this rhyme include *sat, had, men,* and *king*.

Humpty Dumpty Puzzle

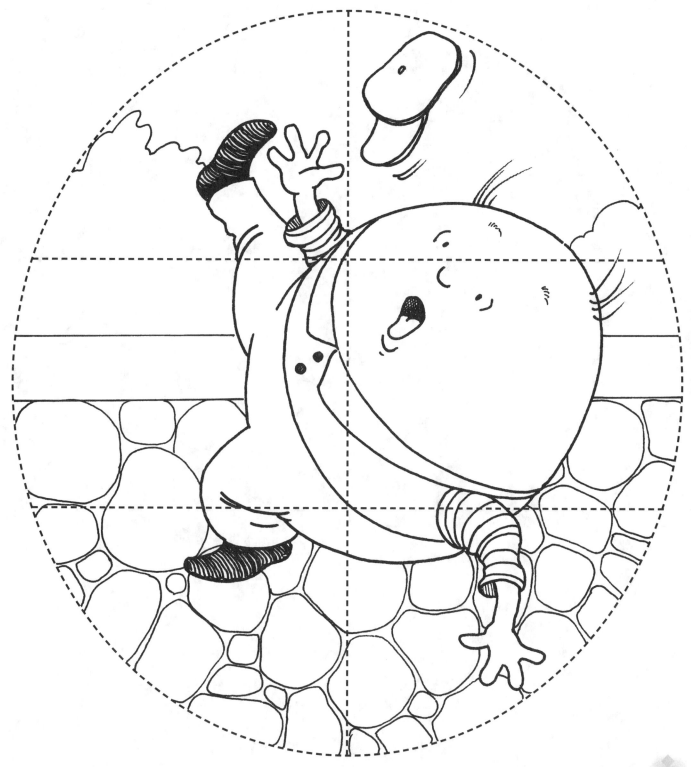

Humpty Dumpty Game Board

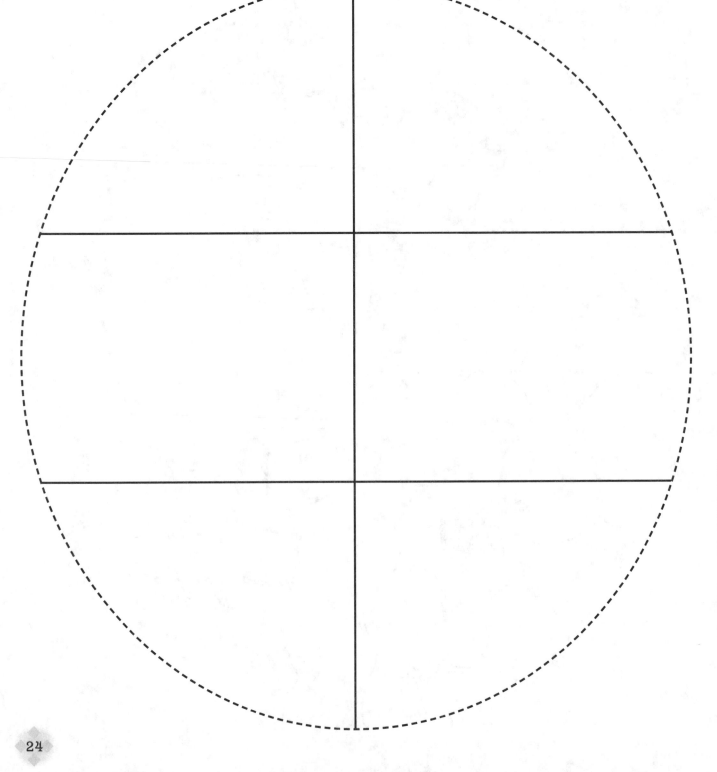

Mother Goose Phonics

Scholastic Professional Books

Bow-Wow

Bow-wow, says the dog.
Meow-meow, says the cat.
Grunt-grunt goes the hog,
And squeak goes the rat.
Buzz-buzz says the bee.
Tweet-tweet says the jay.
Caw-caw, says the crow.
Quack-quack, says the duck,
And what the cuckoo says, you know!

Bow-Wow

SKILL

initial consonants

MATERIALS

- ★ chart paper
- ★ markers (black and other colors)
- ★ animal cards, pages 28–29
- ★ crayons
- ★ empty tissue box
- ★ 5 or 6 large rubber bands
- ★ scissors
- ★ 16 small unlined index cards, cut in half
- ★ glue stick

Getting Ready

1 Photocopy the poem on page 25 for each child, and write the poem on chart paper using a black marker.

2 Copy and cut out the animal cards. Glue each animal card to half an index card. Invite children to color the animals, if desired. Then write the animal's name on the back of each card.

3 Place the tissue box on its side. Remove the plastic around the opening. Then wrap several rubber bands around the opening, spacing them evenly to make "bars." (Use brightly colored ones for a decorative effect.) Use markers to decorate the box to resemble a zoo, as shown. Glue extra copies of a few of the animal cards onto the box, if desired.

Reading the Rhyme

1 Read aloud the nursery rhyme, then invite children to take turns reading aloud each line. As they say the sound each animal makes, encourage children to pretend they are the animal and say the sound as the animal might.

2 Tell children that you're going to read the poem again. Ask them to listen and look carefully for animal-sound words or animal names that begin with consonant letters.

3 After a later reading, ask children to look at their copy of the rhyme and use a crayon to underline any animal-sound words or animal names that begin with consonants. Then let children take turns using a colored marker to underline these initial consonants in the poem on the chart.

4 Ask children if they can think of other sounds that different animals make. (See the examples on page 27.) Let classmates try to guess the animal that makes each sound. List these on the chalkboard or on another sheet of chart paper. Invite children to use the list to add to the nursery rhyme.

Consonant Zoo

1 Show children the Consonant Zoo. Explain that this zoo is so new that it does not yet have any animals. Their job is to go on a safari—a special trip to find animals to put in the zoo.

2 Hold up an animal card. Then invite children to join in with you as you say, "We're on a safari. We found a /t/—tiger." Call on a volunteer to say the letter the animal name begins with and write it on the chalkboard. The child who gives the answer adds the animal card to the zoo. Continue playing until all the animal cards have been placed in the zoo.

Extending Learning

Animal Alphabet Big Book On a large sheet of construction paper, have each child illustrate an animal and the letter its name begins with. Try to include at least one animal for each letter of the alphabet. (See the animals listed on pages 28–29. Animals whose names begin with vowels are listed below. The alphabet book series by Jerry Pallota [Charlesbridge Publishing] is also an excellent source for ideas. Books in this series include *The Icky Bug Alphabet Book, The Bird Alphabet Book*, and *The Furry Alphabet Book*.) Ask each child to write or dictate a sentence about the animal, using words that begin with the same initial letter. (For example, *The lion likes to eat lox and licorice.*) Then make a tagboard cover and help children put the pages in order, punch holes on the left side, and bind with string, ribbon, or O-rings.

A ant, armadillo	**O** owl, ostrich, owl, otter, ox
E eel, elephant	**U** unicorn
I inchworm, iguana	

Name the Animal Riddles Invite children to work in small groups and make up riddles about different animals whose names begin or end with a consonant. For example, "I swim in the sea. My name begins with /f/. What am I?" (fish) As a variation, have children take turns picking animal cards from the Consonant Zoo. Then, keeping the card hidden, they make up a riddle about the animal.

❖ Animal-Sound Words ❖

baa-baa (sheep)	honk-honk (goose)	rippit-rippit (frog)
cheep-cheep (chick)	moo-moo (cow)	roar-roar (lion)
cluck-cluck (chicken)	neigh-neigh (horse)	coo-coo (dove)
hiss-hiss (snake)	oink-oink (pig)	chirp-chirp (cricket)

Animal Cards

Mother Goose Phonics   Scholastic Professional Books

Animal names, left to right:
bat, bear, bee, cat, cow, dog, duck, fish, frog, goat, grasshopper, horse, jellyfish, kangaroo, leopard, lion

Animal Cards

Animal names, left to right:
monkey, mouse, newt, pig, quail, rabbit, raccoon, seal, snake, tiger, turtle, vulture, whale, worm, yak, zebra

Mother Goose Phonics   Scholastic Professional Books

Hickory, Dickory, Dock

Hickory, Dickory, Dock,
The mouse ran up the clock.
The clock struck one,
The mouse ran down.
Hickory, Dickory, Dock.

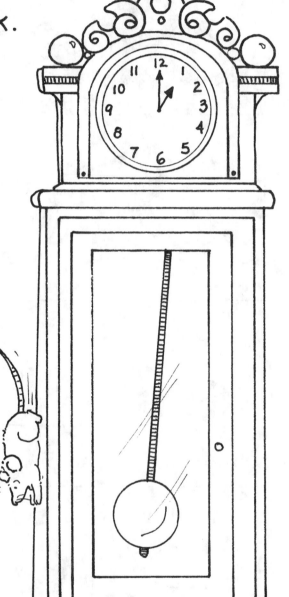

Hickory, Dickory, Dock

Getting Ready

1 Make a copy of the poem on page 30 for each child, and write the poem on chart paper. Underline the *d* in *dock* and the *cl* in *clock* using a colored marker. Underline *-ock* in another color.

2 Photocopy the clock and mouse pattern page for each child.

Reading the Rhyme

1 Read aloud the nursery rhyme once, then reread it, inviting children to use their arms and hands to pantomine the mouse's actions.

2 Before reading the poem again, ask children to name the words that rhyme (*clock* and *dock*). Then ask them to identify ways these two words are alike and different (same *-ock* ending, different beginnings). Cover the beginning and endings of the words to point out these characteristics.

3 Point out the underlined letter *d*. Say the sound /d/ (not *duh*) and ask children to repeat it. Then point out the word family *-ock* and repeat the process. Model how to blend the two sounds together.

4 Repeat this procedure with the underlined blend *cl*. Model how to blend the two letters. Ask children to listen carefully to see if they can hear that each sound in this consonant blend is heard.

5 Invite children to innovate on the rhyme by naming words that end in *-ock* but that begin with a different sound (*lock, rock, sock, block, flock,* and so on). Write these words on self-sticking notes and place over the words *clock* and *dock* in the poem. Then reread the poem with children and invite them to act out the new version.

SKILLS

initial consonants and blends, word families

MATERIALS

★ chart paper
★ markers in different colors
★ self-sticking notes
★ hole punch

For each child:

★ clock and mouse patterns, page 33
★ crayons or markers
★ scissors
★ lightweight cardboard or recycled file folder
★ glue stick
★ 12-inch pipe cleaner or piece of yarn
★ tape

Note: In this book the term consonant blend *is used to describe both the spoken and written form of letter clusters in which each consonant sound is heard.*

Hickory Dickory Consonant Clock

1 Hand out a copy of the pattern page to each child. Invite children to color the patterns. Then have them glue the page to lightweight cardboard and cut out the mouse and the clock. Next, have children punch a hole through each of the circles on the clock and on the mouse.

2 Show children how to thread the pipe cleaner through the clock and the mouse, as shown. The pipe cleaner should appear on the front of the clock but behind the mouse. Have them tape the ends of the pipe cleaner to the back of the clock.

3 Invite children to recite the rhyme as they make the mouse run up the clock by sliding it up the pipe cleaner. Then have children make the mouse climb slowly and read aloud each new word that forms. Ask children to use each word in a sentence.

Extending Learning

Hickory-Dickory-Clock Pocket Chart Copy each line of the nursery rhyme on a strip of tagboard. Places the lines in order in a pocket chart. Then try these activities with your class.

★ Use large self-sticking notes to cover up the last word in each line. Write the missing words on pieces of tagboard, and let children take turns placing the words where they go to complete the poem.

★ Mix up the sentence strips and place them in the pocket chart so that the nursery rhyme is out of order. Invite children to come up to the chart and unscramble the poem, line by line.

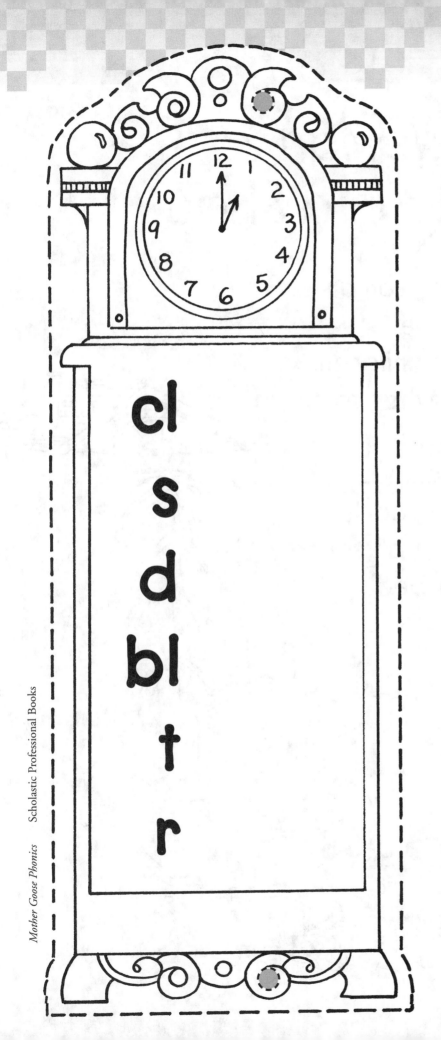

cl
s
d
bl
t
r

Hickory
Dickory
Consonant
Clock

ock

The Old Woman Who Lived in a Shoe

There was an old woman
Who lived in a shoe.
She had so many children,
She didn't know what to do.

She gave them some broth
Along with some bread,
Then hugged them all soundly
And sent them to bed.

The Old Woman Who Lived in a Shoe

Getting Ready

1 Write the poem on chart paper, and make a copy of the poem on page 34 for each child.

2 Copy the shoe pattern pages and glue them to lightweight cardboard. Then cut out the patterns. Invite children to color them. On the back of the shoe, write the name of each picture.

3 Punch a hole through the circles to the right of each consonant blend or digraph. Thread a shoelace through each hole and secure from the back with a knot. (If you use pieces of yarn, wrap the loose yarn ends with tape, or dip in glue and let dry to prevent them from fraying.) Punch a hole through the circles to the left of each picture.

Reading the Rhyme

1 Read aloud the rhyme, then ask children to join in as you read it again. For fun, act out the rhyme with your class. On the floor, create an outline of the Old Woman's shoe using string or yarn. Make sure it is big enough to accommodate all of the children in your class, then tape it down securely. Designate one child to be the Old Woman. Let him or her go around to classmates, pretending to give them broth, bread, and a hug. Then each child in turn goes inside the shoe.

2 Reread the rhyme and focus on the consonant blends. Underline the letters *br* in *broth* and pronounce the blend. Point out that both /b/ and /r/ are heard in this blend. Ask children to search the rhyme for another word that begins with an *r*-blend. (*bread*)

3 On the chalkboard, write other *r*-blends such as *cr, dr, fr, gr, pr,* and *tr.* Ask children to name words that begin with each blend, such as *crow, dress, from, grass, prince,* and *truck,* and list them on the chalkboard.

MATERIALS

- chart paper
- marker
- tape or glue
- ball of string or yarn (optional)
- hole punch or sharp pencil

For each set of cards:

- shoe patterns, pages 37–38
- scissors
- crayons or markers
- glue stick
- lightweight cardboard or recycled file folder
- five 8-inch pieces of shoelace or yarn

Mother Goose Book Nook

There Was an Old Lady Who Lived in a Glove by Bernard Lodge (Whispering Coyote Press, 1992). An old woman who has grown tired of her home in a glove sets out to seek new accommodations. In her travels she meets up with a postman who makes his home in a snail's shell and a dragon that lives in a teapot. Brightly colored woodcuts add a playful appeal to this charming and clever takeoff on the traditional rhyme.

4 Help children notice the digraphs in the rhyme. Underline the letters *th* in *there*, *sh* in *shoe*, *ch* in *children*, and *wh* in *what*, and pronounce each digraph. Explain that each of these consonant pairs stands for one sound. Point out that the letters *ph* form another digraph, as in *photo* and *phonics*. Ask children to find other words in the rhyme that begin with any of these digraphs. (*she, them,* and *then*) Model the sound that each digraph stands for. Also elicit from children that these words all have the letter *h* in common. Then ask children to underline these words in their copy of the rhyme. (Note: If a child says the word *who*, point out that its initial sound is different from other *wh* digraph words.)

Consonant Blend and Digraph Lace-Up Shoes

1 Give one consonant blend shoe pattern to each child. Have children take the attached piece of yarn from the initial consonant blend and match it to the correct picture by pushing the loose end through the hole next to each picture.

2 Repeat the activity using the digraph shoe pattern. Afterward, place the lace-up shoes in a learning center for independent practice. Make additional lace-up shoes using stickers or pictures from old workbooks to give children practice with other consonant blends and digraphs, or blends and digraphs at the end of words.

❖ Mother Goose Learning Center ❖

Blend/Digraph Shoe Sort Collect several old boots or high-top sneakers. Attach to the outside of each a label marked *br, fr, sh, wh, th,* and so on. Create a set of picture cards representing words that begin or end with *r*-blends and digraphs by pasting pictures onto small unlined index cards. (Use the pictures on pages 28–29, stickers, and illustrations from old workbooks.) If you like, first draw a simple outline of a child and then paste each picture inside. Write the name of each picture on the back of the cards, then place them in a basket. Let children visit the center and drop the cards into the correct boot. Children can check themselves by reading the picture name on the back of the cards.

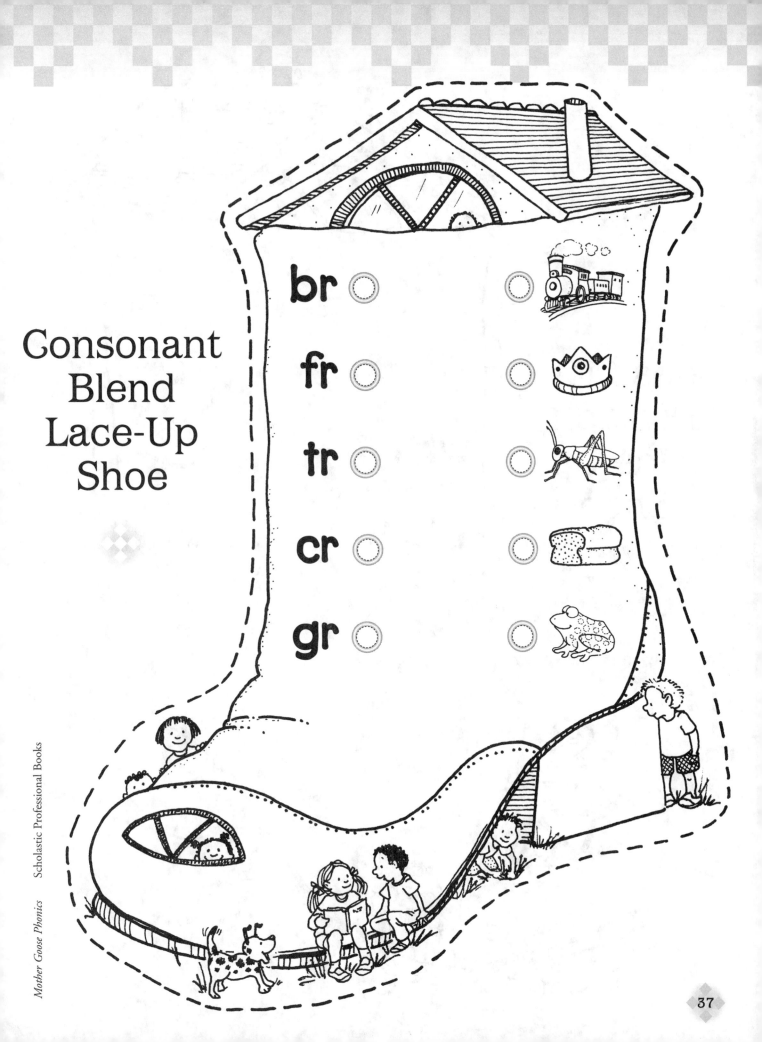

Consonant
Blend
Lace-Up
Shoe

br ○   ○

fr ○   ○

tr ○   ○

cr ○   ○

gr ○   ○

Consonant Digraph Lace-Up Shoe

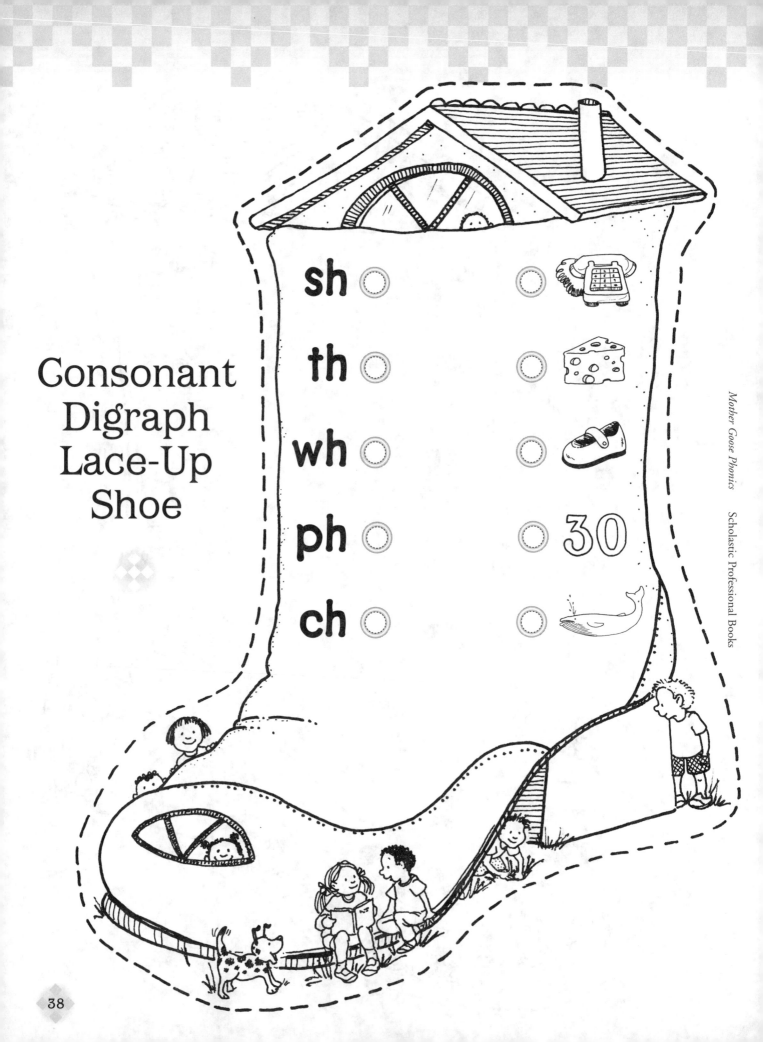

sh ○   ○
th ○   ○
wh ○   ○
ph ○   ○
ch ○   ○

Mother Goose Phonics   Scholastic Professional Books

Mary Had a Little Lamb

Mary had a little lamb,
Its fleece was white as snow.
And everywhere that Mary went,
The lamb was sure to go.

It followed her to school one day,
Which was against the rules.
It made the children laugh and play
To see a lamb at school.

Mary Had a Little Lamb

SKILL

l-blends

MATERIALS

★ chart paper
★ marker
★ self-sticking notes

For each playing pair:

★ Little Lamb game board and markers, page 42
★ lightweight cardboard or recycled file folder (optional)
★ glue stick (optional)
★ crayons or markers
★ scissors
★ spinner, page 22
★ brass fastener
★ paper clip
★ tape

Getting Ready

1 Make a copy of the poem on page 39, and write the poem on chart paper.

2 Photocopy the game board and lamb markers. Glue to lightweight cardboard or laminate for added durability. Color if desired. Then cut out the lamb markers.

3 Photocopy the spinner on page 22. Use a brass fastener and paper clip to assemble it as shown. Write one of the following numbers in each section of the spinner: 1, 2, 3.

Reading the Rhyme

1 Read aloud the rhyme, then invite children to read it with you, singing its familiar tune.

2 Let children take turns personalizing the rhyme, inserting their names instead of *Mary*. They may also enjoy substituting an animal other than a lamb.

3 Ask children if they know or can guess what *fleece* means. Explain that fleece is the wool that grows on a lamb or sheep's body. Underline the *l*-blend at the beginning of this word. Ask children to search the poem for another *l*-blend word (*play*).

4 Generate a list of other *l*-blend words on the chalkboard. For examples, see the list, right. Invite children to change the rhyme even further, this time substituting other *l*-blend words for *fleece* and *play*. For example:

Hannah had a little *bear*.
Its *glove* was white as snow…

…It made the children laugh and *clap*
to see a *bear* at school.

❖ *l*-blend words ❖

black, blew, blink, block, blue
clap, clean, climb, cloud, cluck
flag, flea, flip, floor, flute
glad, glee, glide, glove, glue
plane, please, plink, plow, plump
slam, sled, slip, slow, slump

Little Lamb *l*-Blend Game

1 Give each child a lamb marker, crayons, and tape. Have children color each of the lambs with a different color. Then show them how to fold and tape the lambs to make them stand up.

2 Give a game board to each pair of children. Both players put their lambs on START. The first player spins and moves the number of spaces shown on the spinner, then follows any instructions on the space he or she lands on.

3 When a player lands on a space with a picture, the child must say the name for the picture and then say another word that begins with the same blend. If the child cannot think of a word, he or she moves back to the previous space. Then the next player takes a turn.

4 The game is over when all the players have made it to school. The first player to reach the school is the winner. After playing, put the game in a learning center for children to play independently in pairs or groups.

Extending Learning

Fleecy Lambs Word Wall Help reinforce the *fl*-blend by creating a display filled with fleecy lambs. Provide children with unlined white index cards, cotton balls, white curling ribbon, felt and paper scraps, glue, and crayons. Invite them to use these materials to make a fleecy lamb on their card. Then have children write words that begin with the *fl*-blend beneath the lamb on their card. Use pushpins to display the lambs. Invite children to add to the word wall as they discover new *fl*-blend words.

Make word walls with other words that begin or end with *l*-blends. Provide children with templates to represent different blends (*glove* for *gl*, *cloud* for *cl*, *shield* for *ld*, *belt* for *lt*, and so on).

More Phonics Fun

Challenge children to look for other consonant blends in this rhyme. The words *school* and *snow* contain the *s*-blends *sch* and *sn*. Also help them look for examples of the consonant digraphs *th*, *wh*, and *ch* in *that*, *the*, *white*, and *children*. On the game board, mask the pictures of objects that contain *l*-blends and replace with pictures of objects representing *s*-blends or consonant digraphs.

lamb markers

START

You stop for a snack. Miss 1 turn.

A dog! Watch out! Go back 2 spaces.

You bring Mary her book. Go again.

You stop for a nap. Go back 1 space.

You get lost. Go back 2 spaces.

SCHOOL

Little Lamb
l-Blend Game

Twinkle, Twinkle, Little Star

Twinkle, twinkle, little star,
How I wonder what you are.
Up above the world so high,
Like a diamond in the sky.
Twinkle, twinkle, little star,
How I wonder what you are.

Twinkle, Twinkle, Little Star

SKILL

s-blends

MATERIALS

★ chart paper
★ marker
★ glow-in-the-dark crayons and star stickers (optional)
★ flashlight

For each child or pair:

★ puzzle patterns, pages 46-47
★ scissors
★ envelope
★ white crayons
★ 11- by 17-inch sheet of dark blue or black construction paper
★ glitter
★ glue stick
★ clothesline and clothespins (optional)

Getting Ready

1 Photocopy the poem on page 43 for each child. Use a marker to write the poem on a piece of chart paper. (Or use glow-in-the-dark crayons to write the poem and decorate with glow-in-the-dark stickers, if desired.)

2 Photocopy the pattern pages and cut out the puzzle pieces. Place each set in an envelope.

Reading the Rhyme

1 Dim the lights and invite children to read or sing the rhyme with you as you illuminate each word with a flashlight. Then ask, "What is a diamond?" (a shape, a sparkly gem) Invite children to draw a diamond shape in the air with their fingers (or draw one on the chalkboard).

2 During rereadings, let children take turns shining the flashlight on the words of the poem and leading the rest of the class.

3 Focus on the *s*-blend words in the rhyme, *star* and *sky*. Shine the flashlight on the *s*-blends *st* and *sk* at the beginning of these words.

4 Turn on the lights and give each child a copy of the poem and a crayon. Ask children to search for the *s*-blend words in the rhyme and to draw a diamond around each.

s-Blend Star Puzzlers

1 Give each child or pair of children a set of puzzle pieces, a sheet of dark construction paper, a white or glow-in-the-dark crayon, and a glue stick.

2 Tell children to fold the construction paper in half the short way. Have them label one half "starry" and the other half "sky," underlining the *s*-blend in each word.

3 Have children spread out the puzzle pieces on their desks. Tell them to fill their construction paper sky with stars. To do this, they need to match up the puzzle pieces and glue them to the paper.

4 Have children read the riddles, and assist those who need help. Then tell them to use the riddles and the picture clues to match up their puzzle pieces. Once they have made a match, let them glue the stars with *st* words under <u>starry</u> and those with *sk* words under <u>sky</u>.

5 When they have finished, invite children to decorate their starry skies with glitter and glue. To display children's work, make a class Starry Sky banner by clipping children's papers to a clothesline strung across your classroom.

Look for **Twinkle, Twinkle, Little Star** by Iza Trapani (Whispering Coyote Press, 1994). With ten new verses and vivid illustrations, this rendition of the traditional rhyme follows a little girl as she explores space with the star she has wished upon.

Extending Learning

s-Blend Starry Sky Walk Make a star pattern about six inches wide. (Enlarge the pattern on page 46.) Use it to trace and cut out 16 stars from aluminum foil or gold and silver wrapping paper. Use a marker to write each of the following blends on two stars: *sc, sk, sl, sm, sn, sp, st,* and *sw.* (Or use glow-in-the-dark stars and crayons.) Randomly place the stars in a winding path on the floor, securing them with tape. To play, divide the class into two teams. (Dim the lights if you use glow-in-the-dark stars.) Players take turns rolling a number cube and moving the number of spaces indicated. To stay on a star, players must say a word that begins or ends with the blend on that star, or return to the previous position. The first team to reach the end of the walk wins.

More Phonics Fun

★ Instead of *s*-blends, use this rhyme to let children practice reading words with *r*-controlled vowels, such as *star*. Make another set of star puzzles, substituting these clues.

You knit with this. (yarn)   Animals live here. (farm)
Your hand is part of this. (arm)   This covers a tree trunk. (bark)
This holds things. (jar)   You drive in this. (car)

★ Use "The Itsy Bitsy Spider" (see page 61) to explore other *s*-blend words with your class.

st ove

You cook
on this.

st amp

It goes
on a
letter.

st ool

You sit
on this.

Mother Goose Phonics   Scholastic Professional Books

sk irt

A girl
wears
one.

sk unk

This is
a smelly
animal.

sk ate

You wear
this on
the ice.

Little Bo-Peep

Little Bo-Peep
Has lost her sheep,
And doesn't know where to find them.
Leave them alone, and they'll come home,
Wagging their tails behind them.

Little Bo-Peep

Getting Ready

1 Photocopy the poem on page 48 for each child, and write the poem on chart paper.

2 Make a copy of the Bo-Peep pattern page for each child.

Reading the Rhyme

1 Read aloud the rhyme. Ask children where they think Bo-Peep has lost her sheep. How might she find them?

2 Reread the poem and ask children to listen for words that contain the long-*e* sound in *Peep*. Ask children to identify the words they find. Underline the long-*e* spelling patterns in the rhyme. (-*ea* in *leave*, -*ee* in *Peep* and *sheep*, and -*e* in *she*). Also list these on the chalkboard.

3 Ask children how these words are alike. (They all have the /$\bar{e}$/ sound.) How are they different? (The long-*e* sound is spelled in different ways.)

4 Ask children to think of other words that have the long-*e* sound. List these on the chalkboard. Group together words that share the same word family (phonogram). For examples, see the list below.

❖ Long-e Word Families ❖

		Other Long-e Word Families
-e: me, he, be, she	**-ee:** bee, free, three, tree	-ead, -eak, -ear,
-ea: pea, sea, tea, flea	**-eek:** week, cheek, peek, seek	-ease, -east, -eath,
-each: peach, reach, teach, beach	**-eed:** seed, weed, need, feed	-eave, -eech, -eel,
-eal: meal, seal, heal, real	**-een:** queen, green, screen, teen	-eem, -eer
-eam: beam, team, dream, cream	**-eep:** beep, jeep, peep, sleep	
-ean: bean, Jean, clean, lean	**-eet:** beet, feet, street, sweet	
-eap: heap, leap, cheap, reap	**-eeze:** breeze, sneeze, freeze, squeeze	
-eat: beat, heat, seat, treat		

Bo-Peep Pull-Through

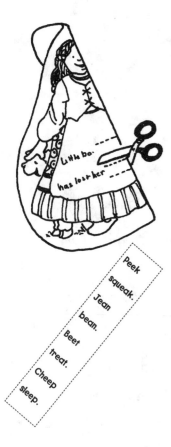

1 Give each child a copy of the pattern page, scissors, and tape. (Let children glue the page to lightweight cardboard for added durability.) Have them cut out Bo-Peep and the word strip. Then show them how to cut two sets of slits in Bo-Peep, as shown. (An easy way to cut the slits is to fold the paper at a right angle to the dotted lines. Then snip along the lines from the crease of the fold inward.) Invite children to color Bo-Peep, if they wish.

2 Model how to put the pull-through together. Turn Bo-Peep facedown and weave the strip in and out of the slits.

3 Tell children to gently pull the strip to reveal the first two long-*e* words, *Cheep* and *sleep*. Ask children to read aloud the two lines.

4 Tell children to pull the strip until a new pair of rhyming long-*e* words appears. Then give them time to use their pull-throughs, read the new words that appear, and share their new, silly versions of the rhyme. Discuss word pairs that have the same and different long-*e* spelling patterns.

5 To give children practice reading other long-*e* word families, make additional copies of the strips, masking out the printed words and substituting new word pairs. (See the list on page 49 for other words with long-*e* word families.)

Extending Learning

Find Bo-Peep's Sheep! Make sheep face patterns by letting children trace one of their hands on a sheet of construction paper, keeping the middle three fingers together. The thumb and pinkie should be outstretched slightly. Then have them cut out the shape, glue cotton balls to the ears, and glue on wiggle eyes, if desired. On each sheep, write words with different long-*e* word families. Before children arrive for school, or while they're at lunch or recess, hide the sheep around the room. Later, invite children to search the room and find Bo-Peep's lost sheep. When they find a sheep, ask them to read the word and use it in a sentence.

More Phonics Fun

"Little Bo-Peep" can also be used to teach consonant digraphs. (See page 35.) Examples in this rhyme include *sheep, where, them,* and *their.*

Bo-Peep
Pull-Through

Little Bo-

has lost her

Peek squeak. Jean bean. Beet treat. Cheep sleep.

Sing a Song of Sixpence

Sing a song of sixpence,
A pocket full of rye;
Four and twenty blackbirds
Baked in a pie.

When the pie was opened,
The birds began to sing;
Wasn't that a dainty dish
To set before the King?

The King was in his counting house,
Counting out his money;
The Queen was in the parlor,
Eating bread and honey.

The maid was in the garden,
Hanging out the clothes;
When down came a blackbird
And pecked off her nose.

Sing a Song of Sixpence

Getting Ready

1 Make a photocopy of the poem on page 52 for each child, and write the poem on chart paper.

2 Make copies of the clothing patterns and cut them out. Invite children to color them. Then tape a penny to the back of each pattern as shown. (The penny works as a counterweight and helps the pieces of clothing hang straight down when clipped to the clothesline.)

3 Write one vowel on each clothespin to correspond with the missing letter of each word on the clothing patterns. (Make sure the vowels read correctly when the clothespins are clipped to the pieces of clothing.) Place the patterns with missing long and short vowels in separate baskets. Put the clothespins in another basket.

4 Tie a length of string or yarn, about 1 1/2 yards long, between two chairs. Or stretch a longer piece across a corner of your classroom and securely tape each end to the wall.

Reading the Rhyme

1 Give each child a copy of the poem. Read the poem aloud. Ask children what they think *sixpence* means (six pennies). Also discuss other unfamiliar vocabulary such as *rye, four and twenty,* and so on.

2 Reread the poem and invite children to read along with you as volunteers act out each verse.

3 Tell children that you are going to read the poem again. Ask them to listen for words that contain the short-*i* sound, as in *sing.* Label a column "short *i*" and list these words underneath. (*sing, king, sixpence, in, dish, his*) Repeat this process with long *i* (point out the different spellings of long *i* in *pie* and *rye*), then short and long *a, e,* and *o*. (There are no short- or long-*u* sounds in the rhyme; the word *full* contains a variant vowel sound.)

4 Have children look at the word lists. Ask them to add more words to each list.

SKILLS

short and long vowels

MATERIALS

★ chart paper
★ marker
★ ball of yarn or string

For each playing group:

★ clothing patterns, pages 55–56
★ crayons or markers
★ 10 pennies
★ tape
★ 10 spring-type clothespins
★ 3 small baskets

Vowel Clothes Clip-Ups

1 Tell children that they are going to hang up clothes just as the maid did in the nursery rhyme. First, have children take turns forming words with short vowels. To do this, they will pick an article of clothing from the short-vowel basket, clip the correct vowel clothespin to the blank space in each word, then read the word aloud.

2 After working with short vowels, switch baskets and have children practice forming words with long vowels.

3 Put the materials for this activity in a learning center so that children can continue to work on long and short vowels independently. Make the activity self-correcting by writing the answers ("short *a*," "long *i*," and so on) on the back of each pattern.

Mother Goose Learning Center

Four-and-Twenty-Blackbirds Pie Let children continue working with long and short vowels. Cut a "slice" out of a paper plate. Place it face to face with another plate. Staple the plates together. Color or decorate the "pie." Make 24 black construction paper birds (big enough to fit inside the pie). Use a white crayon to write 12 words with long vowels on half of the birds and 12 short-vowel words on the remainder. (Focus on one vowel, such as *a*, or mix different vowels.) Make the activity self-correcting by writing "long *a*" or "short *a*" on the back of each bird. Put the birds inside the pie, word-side up. Invite children to let the birds out and place them on a "long-*a*" or "short-*a*" plate, according to the sounds the words contain.

More Phonics Fun

Give children practice with other long- and short-vowel words. Make extra copies of the clothing patterns, masking out the letters printed on each. Write words on each pattern, leaving a blank space for the missing letter or letters. (Try masking out vowel digraphs such as *ea* in *eat*, *ai* in *paid*, and *oa* in *toast*.)

You might also have children search the poem for words with diphthongs (*ou, ow, oi, ou*) and make a set of clothing patterns to help them practice these skills. Examples of words with diphthongs in this rhyme include *counting, house, out*, and *down*.

k_te

_at

n_se

b_ke

Vowel Clothes
Clip-Ups

th__t

p__ck

s__ng

j__b

f__n

c__be

Vowel
Clothes
Clip-Ups

Mother Goose Phonics Scholastic Professional Books

Mistress Mary

Mary, Mary, quite contrary,
How does your garden grow?
With silver bells and cockle shells,
And pretty maids all in a row.

Mistress Mary

MATERIALS

* chart paper
* marker

For each child:

* flower pot and flower patterns, page 60 (2 per child)
* lightweight cardboard
* glue stick
* scissors
* crayons or markers

Getting Ready

1 Make a photocopy of the poem on page 57 for each child, and write the poem on chart paper.

2 Photocopy two copies of the flower pot and flower pattern page for each child. Glue the patterns to lightweight cardboard for added durability. Cut out the flowers and the pots. Make slits in the pots as indicated.

3 Write "short *o*" on one pot and "long *o*" on the other. Then write one word from the lists below on each of the flowers. (Write the vowel sound on the back of each flower for children to self-check.) Make three short-*o* flowers and three long-*o* flowers.

long o: *grow, row, low, mow, know, fold, coat, road, coal, robe, note, home, soak, toast, roll, poll, most, rose, ghost, hope*

short o: *job, hot, drop, log, rod, job, pond, hop, top, fox, dot, got, knot, sock, nod, romp, rock, chop, mop, smock*

Reading the Rhyme

1 Read aloud the rhyme with children. Discuss words that may be unfamiliar to children, such as *contrary*. Ask children if they think the flowers in this garden are real or imaginary.

2 Read aloud the rhyme again, substituting the names of children in your class for *Mary*. When you reach the third line in the rhyme, invite the child whose name is being used to tell the kinds of flowers—real or imaginary—that are growing in his or her garden.

3 During a rereading, ask children to listen for the long-*o* words in the poem. (*grow* and *row*) Write these words on the chalkboard. Then ask children to name other words that contain the long-*o* sound, and list them too.

4 Help children explore the short-*o* sound. Say the word *shop* and point out that it contains /ŏ/. Write another version of the rhyme (at left) on the chalkboard, then read it aloud.

Ask volunteers to take turns circling words in the revised poem with the short-*o* sound. Then generate a list of other words with the short-*o* sound.

Mary, Mary, quite contrary,
What's in your flower shop?
Daisies with dots and
    forget-me-nots,
All lined up in flower pots.

Grow a Vowel Garden

1 Give each child a set of two flower pots, a set of six flowers, and crayons. Invite children to color lightly the pots and the flowers.

2 Tell children that they are going to grow a vowel garden. Have children slide each of the flowers into the correct flower pot based on its short- or long-*o* sound.

Mother Goose Learning Center

Vowel Garden Interactive Bulletin Board Let children continue to practice long and short vowels. On a large sheet of chart paper, draw two planting rows. At the start of each row, tack up an index card "plant marker" on which you've written a vowel sound (short *o*/ long *o*, short *e*/long *e*, and so on). Write an assortment of long- and short-vowel words on flower patterns (see page 60), or use pictures representing these words. Place the flowers in a basket. Invite children to visit the center and use pushpins to "plant" flowers in the correct rows. Note: Instead of short and long vowels, you might draw five planting rows and have children practice planting flowers with words that represent each of the long or short vowel sounds.

More Phonics Fun

Repeat the Grow a Vowel Garden activity but this time write "short *e*" on one flower pot and "long *e*" on the other. Then use the word lists below to prepare a new set of flower patterns.

long e: *heap, feel, street, free, cream, sea, bead, weak, meal, bee, green, heat, bean, team, flea, seat, seal, Jean, tea, feast*

short e: *shell, bell, well, bed, left, stem, bend, fence, dress, west, next, pet, belt, fell, bench, less, shelf, wed, neck, held*

Grow a Vowel Garden

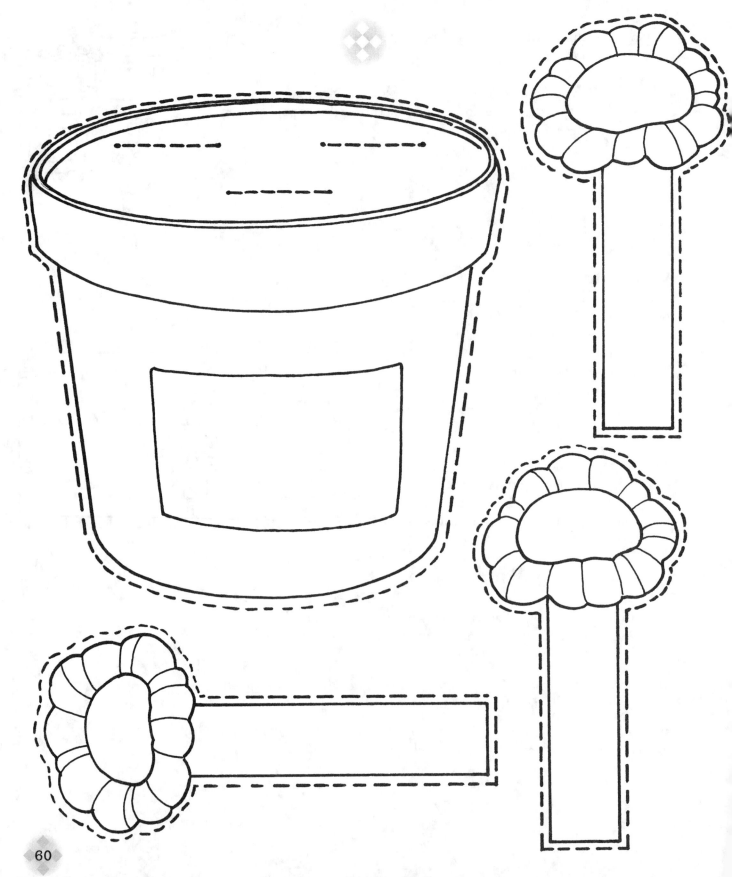

The Itsy Bitsy Spider

The itsy bitsy spider
Climbed up the water spout.
Down came the rain
And washed the spider out.
Out came the sun
And dried up all the rain.
And the itsy bitsy spider
Climbed up the spout again.

The Itsy Bitsy Spider

MATERIALS

★ chart paper
★ marker
★ hole punch

For each child:

★ spider slider spout pattern, page 64
★ spider pattern, below
★ scissors
★ crayons or markers
★ 12-inch pipe cleaner or piece of yarn
★ tape or gluestick

spider pattern

Getting Ready

1 Write the rhyme on chart paper, and make a copy of the poem on page 61 for each child.

2 Make a copy of the spider slider spout pattern for each child. Also copy the spider pattern (below) for each child.

Reading the Rhyme

1 Read or sing the rhyme aloud, and then invite children to act it out using the traditional fingerplay motions.

2 Underline the words in the rhyme that contain the vowel diphthongs *ou* and *ow* (*spout, down,* and *out*). Ask children how these words are alike. (They all contain the /ou/ sound.) Point out that these words share the same sound but that sound is spelled differently.

3 Ask children to name other words that have the /ou/ sound. List these on the chalkboard. Then challenge them to come up with a variation of "The Itsy Bitsy Spider" using two of the words on the list. For example:

The itsy bitsy spider went into the town.
On the way there, she met a funny clown.

The itsy bitsy spider crawled along the ground.
A tasty bug for lunch is what she found!

Spider Slider Spout

1 Give each child a copy of the spider slider spout pattern page and spider pattern. Have children cut out the patterns along the dotted lines. Then have them cut the spout pattern in half along the center dotted line.

2 Show children how to cut along the dotted lines to make five flaps in the water spout.

3 Tell children to place the water spout pattern on top of the piece with the pictures. Have them line up the patterns and tape or glue around the edges to seal them together, leaving the flaps free.

Mother Goose Book Nook

The Itsy Bitsy Spider by Iza Trapani (Whispering Coyote Press, 1993). Author-illustrator Trapani adds five lively new verses to the familiar song about a determined little spider.

....

Young children will adore Lorianne Siomades's wild, wacky, and colorfully exuberant version of **The Itsy Bitsy Spider** (Boyds Mills Press, 1999).

4 Have children punch a hole through each of the circles on the spout and on the spider. Then show them how to thread the spider through the pipe cleaner, poke the ends of the pipe cleaner through the holes on the spout, bend down the ends, and tape to the back.

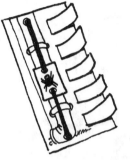

5 Invite children to read or sing aloud the rhyme as they slide the spider up the water spout. Explain that the spider will see different things as it climbs. It will see only things whose names contain the same /ou/ sound as *spout*. Ask children to open the first flap at the bottom and read the two words inside. Ask: "Would the spider see *snow* or an *owl*? Which word has the same /ou/ sound as *spout*?" (*owl*) Have children color the picture.

6 Let children continue sliding the spider up the spout, opening each flap, and coloring the picture with the /ou/ sound in each pair.

Mother Goose Learning Center

Diphthong Spiderwebs Use lengths of string and pushpins to create a spiderweb on a bulletin board. Draw a simple spider shape on small index cards, cut in half. (Or enlarge and trace the spider pattern on page 62.) Write words with the /ou/ sound on half of the cards. (See the list below.) Also prepare cards with words that do not contain diphthongs but that have similar spellings and are pronounced differently. Examples include *show, blow, snow, grow, crow, throw, you, young, moon, rose, no, coat,* and *clock.* Place the cards in a bag and attach below the web with a pushpin. Invite children to visit the center and use pushpins to place word cards on the web that have the /ou/ sound.

words with /ou/ diphthong: *cow, now, gown, owl, brown, frown, out, count, now, mouth, clown, down, how, shout, mouse, house*

Spider Slider Spout

(Outside) **(Inside)**

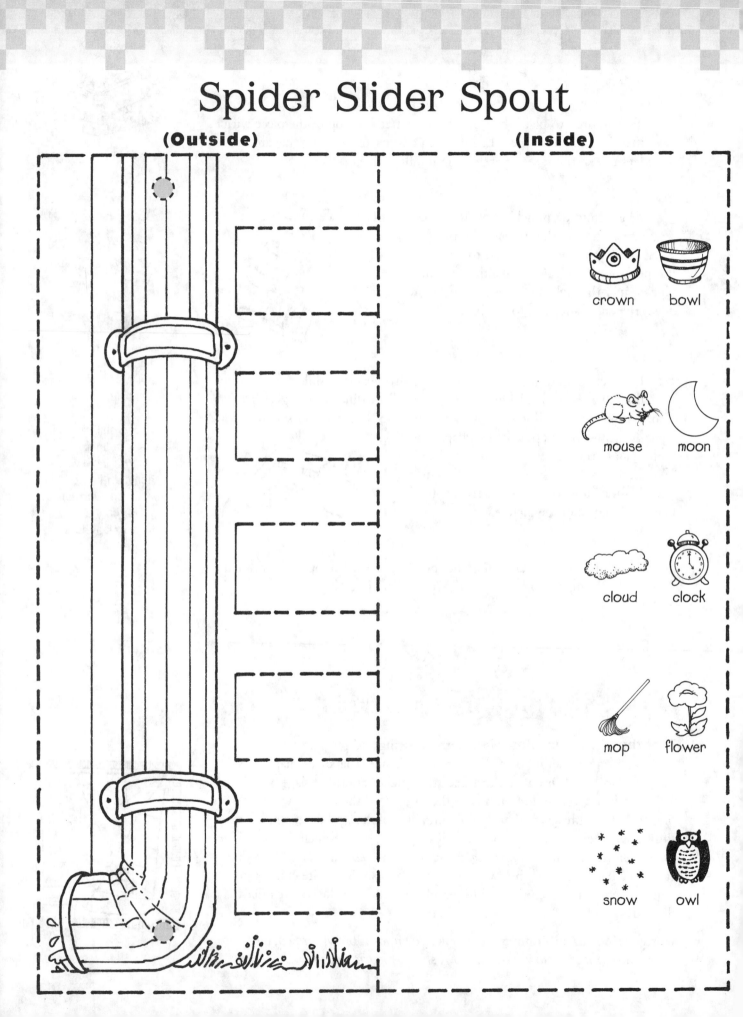

crown   bowl

mouse   moon

cloud   clock

mop   flower

snow   owl